Thirteen
of Reve

GW00374352

ex libris

Candlestick Press

Published by:
Candlestick Press,
DiVersity House, 72 Nottingham Road,
Arnold, Nottingham NG5 6LF
www.candlestickpress.co.uk

Design, typesetting, print and production by DiVersity Creative
Marketing Solutions Ltd., www.diversity-nottm.co.uk

Introduction © Sophie Hannah, 2012

Illustrations © Cary Swann, 2012

© Candlestick Press, 2012

ISBN: 978 1 907598 13 5

Acknowledgements:
Candlestick Press thanks Sophie Hannah for her Introduction and for
her poem 'If You Were Standing Where His Shadow Fell' written for
this pamphlet. Thanks are also due to *14 Magazine* and Jack Powers
for permission to re-print 'Curse of a Boyfriend Scorned' which first
appeared in *14 Magazine, Issue 11*; Gill Learner and *Obsessed with
Pipework* for 'Ties' which first appeared in *Obsessed with Pipework,
Issue 43,* Summer 2008; Gregory Woods and Carcanet Press for 'Lady
van der Meer's Win' from 'Quidnunc', published in *Quidnunc,*
Carcanet Press, 2007; Bloodaxe Books for 'Bitcherel' © Eleanor
Brown, published in *Maiden Speech,* Bloodaxe Books, 1996; Stephen
Dobyns for 'Spite' from *Velocities, New and Selected Poems
1966-1992,* Penguin, 1994; Roz Goddard and Nine Arches Press for
'Janice' from *The Soprano Sonnets and Other Poems,* Nine Arches
Press, 2010; Lorraine Mariner and Picador Poetry, an imprint of Pan
Macmillan, for 'There is nothing wrong with my sister' © Lorraine
Mariner, from *Furniture,* Picador Poetry, 2009; Kit Wright for 'My
Version' from *Hoping It Might Be So, Poems 1974-2000,* Leviathan,
2000; Christine Webb and Grey Hen Press for 'You Took My Space'
© Christine Webb, from *A Twist of Malice,* Grey Hen Press, 2008;
Martin Hayes and Redbeck Press for 'Alex', © Martin Hayes, from
Letting Loose the Hounds, Redbeck Press, 2001; Robin Vaughan-
Williams and Happen*Stance* for 'MANAGER #10 Fired!' © Robin
Vaughan-Williams, from *The Manager,* Happen*Stance*, 2010; Faber
& Faber for 'Spring Onions' © Wendy Cope from 'From June to
December', *Making Cocoa for Kingsley Amis,* Faber & Faber, 1986.
'Thought for a Sunshiny Morning' by Dorothy Parker is reproduced by
permission of Gerald Duckworth and Co. Ltd.

Where poets are no longer living, their dates are given.

Spring Onions

Decapitating the spring onions,
She made this mental note:
You can tell it's love, the real thing,
When you dream of slitting his throat.

Wendy Cope

Late Last Night

Late last night I slew my wife,
Stretched her on the parquet flooring,
I was loath to take her life,
But I had to stop her snoring.

Harry Graham (1874 – 1936)

Thought for a Sunshiny Morning

It costs me never a stab nor squirm
To tread by chance upon a worm.
"Aha, my little dear," I say,
"Your clan will pay me back one day."

Dorothy Parker (1893 – 1967)

Introduction

Revenge is unique among abstract commodities. All of us, at some point in our lives, yearn for it - some of us many times; some of us only once, but that once might last a lifetime - but it is probably in the best interests of our good characters if we never get it. Revenge, so perfect and tempting in our minds, diminishes us if we turn it from an idea into a successfully performed action. In that respect, it is rather like eating certain well known fast-food-chain cheeseburgers: you feel revolting immediately afterwards. Revenge is a dish best never served at all, but merely fantasised about.

Which is probably why some wise person or other said, 'The best revenge is living well'. Whoever invented this motto clearly hadn't heard the urban legend about the woman who sewed prawns into the curtain linings of the boyfriend who jilted her. Even someone as enlightened as the Dalai Lama would have to admit that, as revenges go, that one's pretty cool.

In fact, the best revenge is the one that life provides spontaneously, without our having to sully ourselves. When I was 15, my so-called friend Jackie spent an entire evening snogging the divine Justin Taylor - a boy I had invited to this particular party because I wanted to snog him myself, as Jackie well knew. The minute Justin left, she rushed over to me, gushing, 'I'm sorry! I'm sorry! We're not going to fall out over this, are we?'. I pretended to forgive her (largely because I'd consoled myself by snogging the also-rather-gorgeous Joel Nally in the interim), but I can't pretend I wasn't delighted when Justin's girlfriend Dawn - whose existence neither Jackie nor I had been aware of - turned up at our school the next day and punched Jackie in the face. Incidents like this are the reason I find the arguments of atheists like Richard Dawkins unconvincing.

When my poetry publisher, Carcanet Press, reopened their offices after the IRA bombing of Manchester in 1995, writer and academic Gerald Hammond delivered a rousing speech, one line of which I will never forget: 'Some try to change the world with bombs, others with poems.' At which point the poet Steven Blyth whispered in my ear, 'Surely there's some kind of middle way?'.

There is: you buy a little anthology of poems about revenge (this one, for example) and give it as a present to the person who has wronged you. If they misinterpret your kind gift as a veiled attack, look hurt and say, 'How can you think that?' They won't be able to prove anything.

Sophie Hannah

Curse of a Boyfriend Scorned

May you stub your toe, ding your elbow
on the doorframe, knock your knee on the computer desk,
crack the shell of a cavity on bacon gristle,
get a blistering sunburn on the first day of spring.

May your children be pigeon-toed and math-challenged,
your husband suffer from high cholesterol and rotor cuff tears,
your mother become forgetful before her time, your sister
marry a know-it-all who talks too loud at Christmas dinner.

May you forget why you chose someone else, why he seemed
funnier, handsomer – a more promising prospect. May you stop
on a day like today when gray clouds cover the sun and ask
if life may have been perfect on a different path. 'Til then

may your cat have hairballs, may your basement leak, may you
wander the house wondering what it was you set out to do.

Jack Powers

Bitcherel

You ask what I think of your new acquisition;
and since we are now to be 'friends',
I'll strive to the full to cement my position
with honesty. Dear – it depends.

It depends upon taste, which must not be disputed;
for which of us *does* understand
why some like their furnishings pallid and muted,
their cookery wholesome, but bland?

There isn't a *law* that a face should have features,
it's just that they generally *do*;
God couldn't give colour to all of his creatures,
and only gave wit to a few;

I'm sure she has qualities, much underrated,
that compensate amply for this,
along with a charm that is so understated
it's easy for people to miss.

And if there are some who choose clothing to flatter
what beauties they think they possess,
when what's underneath has no shape, does it matter
if there is no shape to the dress?

It's not that I think she is *boring* precisely,
that isn't the word I would choose;
I know there are men who like girls who talk nicely
and always wear sensible shoes.

It's not that I think she is vapid and silly;
it's not that her voice makes me wince;
but – chilli con carne without any chilli
is only a plateful of mince...

Eleanor Brown

Ties

It mocks me *sotto voce* from the wardrobe;
out, it is a jazz of orange stripes.
You wore it once to kick
against convention, haven't put it on
for years. It was a present from the woman
we don't talk about.

I grip the scissors, slip the lower blade
inside the silky point and press until
my arm is fully stretched. Threads part,
warp and weft in one long sweep,
facings and linings lie revealed. The sound
is like a long-held sigh.

What next? The old school falls
in a blue-gold tangle; on top writhe
regimental snakes. Tired of the lisp of silk,
I reach for polyester, the company-logo'd red;
the sibilance is higher. Knitted wool needs snips
as deep as groans.

This is a serenade for scissors,
but what part for Harris tweed?
It's tough and growls as the right arm drops;
lapels show their teeth. Gaberdine
rasps from vent to nape, linen has crunch,
waxed cloth whines.

Now I need the purr of cashmere
with its smell of some elusive thing
I do not like. But it's Tuesday and the Club
straight from the office; you're wearing it
and won't be home till late.
Well, I can wait.

Gill Learner

Lady van der Meer's Win

She bided what was left
of what was once her time
with one eye on the clock,
the other on that less
than nothing, lower than
the belly of a snake,
her lifelong enemy
the Duchess of Deceit.
Not till the stroke of twelve,
and then not till the twelfth
had played its echo out
around the gilded dome,
did Lady van der Meer
let slip the chance remark
rehearsing which had kept
her out of circulation
and out of harm for weeks.
So long indeed had she
been gone that there were those
who hardly recognised her
but by the rubies at
her throat and the revenge
implicit in her glare.
The husband at her side
was barely visible,
his small-talk audible
only to those for whom
the insignificant
holds weight: diplomacy,
the game of empire, the
sad likelihood of war…

The rest had but to wait
and curiosity
would be rewarded with
whatever came to pass –
defeat or victory.
In the event – for an
event it was – the wit
of one was parried by
the other with a smirk,
as if a duchess could
by dint of blood alone
shrug off the paramount
necessity of face.
A pin was heard to drop,
a curl came loose, and we
self-consciously went back
to Monsieur Vaudet's pudding,
that miracle of sweetness
half tamed by bitterness.

Gregory Woods

Spite

I steal your mailbox, leave
gum on your sidewalk. I
seduce your sister, ignore your wife.
I tear one page from each of your books.
I convince you that I am your friend.

When people ask about you,
I shake my head. When they
tell about you, I nod.

Today, I hang myself
from a greased flagpole
outside your picture window.
Yesterday, I stole your curtains.

Stephen Dobyns

The Criminal

One was a female, who had grievous ill
Wrought in revenge, and she enjoy'd it still:
With death before her, and her fate in view,
Unsated vengeance in her bosom grew:
Sullen she was and threat'ning; in her eye
Glared the stern triumph that she dared to die:
But first a being in the world must leave –
'Twas once reproach; 'twas now a short reprieve.
She was a pauper bound, who early gave
Her mind to vice, and doubly was a slave;
Upbraided, beaten, held by rough control,
Revenge sustain'd, inspired, and fill'd her soul.
She fired a full-stored barn, confess'd the fact,
And laugh'd at law and justified the act:
Our gentle vicar tried his powers in vain,
She answer'd not, or answer'd with disdain;
Th' approaching fate she heard without a sigh,
And neither cared to live nor fear'd to die.

George Crabbe (1754 – 1832)

If You Were Standing Where His Shadow Fell

The tyrant's favourite chocolates are Maltesers.
We roll them at his toes, submerge his feet.
Some drop through grates; we pluck them out with tweezers.
He sulks. They are too round and brown and sweet.

The tyrant thinks a soppy armadillo
would make an ideal pet: tough shell, limp heart.
He keeps a doodle underneath his pillow.
The rest is down to us. He's done his part;

we have to find it, buy it, love it, feed it,
teach it that we're its slaves, ignore the swell
of indignation, since we'll never need it.
If you were standing where his shadow fell

you'd willingly succumb to his distortions.
You'd contemplate revenge, then rule it out.
He's living what he's earned, in hefty portions:
each day, each year. Oh, he is in no doubt

that we confide in lamps, bond with umbrellas,
in preference to him. This is our fault,
or so he thinks, confining us to cellars.
He will die unaware. Exalt! Exalt

when he releases you; embrace the terror
of his renewed attack before too long.
For your sake and for his, don't make the error
Of showing him he's all the bad and wrong.

Sophie Hannah

Janice

As younger brothers go, you were the pits.
Sticky hand up ma's skirt, dark eyes forever
pooling into innocence like you were
the Madonna's blessed child. I should have
let your pram kiss a thundering truck when
I had the chance, blamed it on the slippery heat,
watched as you flat-lined. I could have altered time.
It would have been my one defining act.

Jesus, I hated those dresses, the shoes –
I wanted to be you, sliding on dad's leather
seats, going out back where the blood was.
I pretended to be a girl, fingers in those curls.
What's running through me is ice and steel;
the more you suffer, the better I feel.

Roz Goddard

There is nothing wrong with my sister

After you told my sister
that there was no one else
but you no longer wanted her,
she went to bed and tried to work out
what she had done
and what was wrong with her
and spent the night awake.

There is nothing wrong with my sister
but may there be something wrong
with the Ikea wardrobe
she helped you to build,
so that tonight it falls apart
and wakes you
from your unaccompanied sleep.

Lorraine Mariner

My Version

I hear that since you left me
Things go from bad to worse,
That the Good Lord, quite rightly,
Has set a signal curse

On you, your house and lover.
(I learn, moreover, he
Proves twice as screwed-up, selfish
And sodden, dear, as me.)

They say your days are tasteless,
Flattened, disjointed, thinned.
Across the waste my absence,
Love's skeleton, has grinned.

Perfect. I trust my sources
Of information are sound?
Or is it just some worthless rumour
I've been spreading round?

Kit Wright

You Took My Space

You took my space
and when I protested
(too politely)
'It's Disabled Parking'
you snarled, 'Too many
bloody Disabled
Spaces' and sped away
into Marks & Spencer's.

In Marks & Spencer's
nothing will fit you
the assistants sneer
as you root through the knickers
laughter follows you
down all the aisles
the food counters
are full of spinach
and frozen cod heads
eyeing you glassily
huge queues snake
back from the checkouts
the cashiers go on strike
a hoaxer shouts Fire
the building is evacuated
someone else's child
is sick in your handbag
and out in the car park
a delivery lorry
has crushed your car
to a dense metal cowpat
before blocking the exit.

Be my guest, madam.

Christine Webb

Alex

after one too many bollockings
in front of the rest of the workforce
after having his wages cut
for time off
even though he'd spent many hours after his shift
helping out
after being told he was on report
and had to ask a supervisor
if it was okay for him to go and have a shit
after being made to do three Saturday shifts a month
when the rest of us done maybe one every two
after hearing that the trainees were now being started
on the same pay he was getting
even though he'd been there for four years
and when he was told on a Friday
that on Monday he was to report
to our new Waterloo office
even though he lived only a half mile
from our Ladbroke Grove office
he decided that he was being singled out
and took a spray can to all the reps' and supervisors' cars
on the walk through the car park
outta there

Martin Hayes

MANAGER #10
Fired!

The manager looks at me.
He says it's time I went.
They won't be needing me any more.

I don't understand.
I want to know why.
But he says some things are better left unsaid.

I tell him I don't want to go.
I've put so much into this job already.
I've been ill, my nose has been running constantly.
I never asked for any sympathy.
Didn't pull a sickie.

Doesn't he realise how vulnerable I am?
I'm a sensitive person.
'I'm a poet,' I say.
'You can't fire me,
I'll put you in a poem.'

'Not a very well known poet,' he says
and fires me anyway.
Some day I will have my revenge.

Robin Vaughan-Williams